KNOWLEDGE ENCYCLOPEDIA
SPACE
DISCOVERIES
INVENTIONS & DISCOVERIES

(An imprint of Prakash Books Pvt. Ltd.)

Wonder House Books

Corporate & Editorial Office
113-A, 1st Floor, Ansari Road,
Daryaganj, New Delhi-110002
Tel +91 11 2324 7062-65

Disclaimer: The information contained in this encyclopedia has been collated with inputs from subject experts. All information contained herein is true to the best of the Publisher's knowledge.

Printed in 2020 in India

ISBN : 9789390391035

Table of Contents

OUT IN **SPACE**

The earliest astronomers mapped the sky by observing it year after year.
They discovered and named the nearest planets, moons, stars and shooting stars, and charted asteroids and galaxies. As our knowledge of the universe increased, scientists realised that all heavenly bodies followed certain rules.

Scientists used these observations, along with a pinch of imagination, and made calculations to decipher the universe. The study of the universe is called **cosmology** and the people who study it are called cosmologists. The study of the physical laws of the universe is called **astrophysics** ('astro' means stars). It is a pioneering branch of science that allows us to explore alien worlds.

▼ *Earth as seen from the Moon*

Cosmology
From Ancient Times to the 19th Century

We have slowly but steadily managed to glean many secrets of the universe over the centuries. The course of cosmology has weathered the pressures of religion and superstition, the suppression of female scientists, the prejudices of class and race and many other odds. Let us take a look at some of the most brilliant champions of this triumphant science.

Anaximander (610–546 BCE)

The first known person to develop a systematic view of the world was the Greek philosopher Anaximander. He was also the person who recognised that Earth moved freely through space. This idea may seem obvious to us now, but most civilisations of the time believed that the planet was upheld by pillars, heroes or beasts. So, he was quite a path-breaker at the time.

▲ *An ancient Roman mosaic depicting Anaximander holding a sundial*

◀ *A 1628 oil painting of the cheerful Democritus, by Dutch artist Hendrick Terbrugghen*

Democritus (460–370 BCE)

Democritus was also known as the 'laughing philosopher'. He believed that the universe was made of tiny particles called atoms. According to him, the universe contained infinite, diverse worlds that followed a set of physical laws rather than the whims of gods. He also worked out that the Milky Way's appearance was caused by the light of stars.

Aristarchus of Samos (310–230 BCE)

In ancient times, people thought Earth was at the centre of the universe. Mathematician Aristarchus first proposed that the Sun was at the centre of the universe. He proposed this model 18 centuries before Nicolaus Copernicus famously did the same.

▶ *A statue of Aristarchus at the Aristotle University of Thessaloniki, Greece*

▲ *Although not the first one to propose the theory, Nicolaus Copernicus (1473–1543) was the man who popularised heliocentrism, which theorises that the planets revolve around the Sun*

⭐ Incredible Individuals

Born a nobleman, Tycho Brahe (1546–1601) was kidnapped and brought up by his uncle. Brahe later refused to take his place at the royal court. Defying his family, he became a scientist. Brahe's work was revolutionary and it changed the way we understand planetary motion and gravity.

▶ A brilliant group of women known as 'Harvard's Computers' made significant contributions to astronomy. Among them were Henrietta Swan Leavitt (1868–1921), Annie Jump Cannon (1863–1941), Williamina Fleming (1857–1911) and Antonia Maury (1866–1952)

▼ The Kepler crater on the Moon is named in honour of Johannes Kepler

Hipparchus (190–120 BCE)

Hipparchus was one of the greatest Greek cosmologists. He was the first to accurately measure the distance between Earth and the Moon. His work revealed the existence of over 850 stars. He also discovered the 'wobbling' of Earth that causes the equinoxes. This is called **precession** and it was the third movement of Earth to be discovered after rotation and revolution.

◀ Almagest, written by Claudius Ptolemy (100–170 CE) was the ultimate guide to thousands of stars and constellations and to the movement of planets for 1500 years

Johannes Kepler (1571–1630)

Blessed with a keen intellect, Kepler propounded the laws of planetary motion. He also discovered that tides occurred because of the Moon. His work on planetary motion led Newton to discover the laws of gravity.

Isaac Newton (1643–1727)

Newton's laws of gravity and motion completely changed our understanding of physics and nature. Newton also invented the first reflecting telescope and showed how sunlight could be split into all the colours of the rainbow.

◀ Isaac Newton was a key figure of Europe's scientific revolution

John Herschel (1792–1871)

Nephew of the brilliant astronomer Caroline Herschel, John did the first global survey of stars. He built the first telescopic lab in the southern hemisphere and catalogued 500 more nebulae and over 3000 double stars. He named seven of Saturn's moons and four of Uranus's moons.

▶ John Herschel took the first-ever photograph on a glass plate. He even coined the word 'photography'

The Space Race

The Second World War ended in 1945. The US and Soviet Union had been allies during this war. But without a common enemy, the capitalist US and the communist Soviet Union soon turned against each other. Instead of clashing openly, they fought to establish their interests in various countries across the globe. This period is known as the Cold War.

🔍 The Space War

One of the few good things to come out of the Cold War was a spate of space-related technologies. In 1955, the US declared that it would launch a satellite into the outer space. The USSR decided to launch its own satellite first. Thus began a fierce competition known as the space race.

▲ Taken at the height of the space race, this photograph shows Soviet leader Nikita Khrushchev with Valentina Tereshkova, the first woman in space and (in the far left) Yuri Gagarin, the first man in space. Between them is Pavel Popovich, another pioneering cosmonaut

4 October, 1957

The USSR becomes the first nation to successfully launch an artificial satellite. It is called Sputnik, a Russian word meaning fellow wanderer.

3 November, 1957

A live animal orbits Earth for the first time on the USSR's satellite Sputnik-2. This is the dog Laika.

◀ In 1958, TIME Magazine portrayed Soviet leader Nikita Khrushchev as the Man of the Year with the satellite Sputnik in his hands

◀ A statue of Laika in her space harness in Moscow, Russia

1960

NASA launches the first successful weather satellite, Tiros-1. Its ability to detect cloud cover and predict hurricanes encourages the development of the Nimbus programme of weather satellites.

29 July, 1958

America establishes the National Aeronautics and Space Administration (NASA) after the success of Sputnik.

▲ NASA Headquarters in Washington D.C.

1 February, 1958

The US successfully launches a satellite called Explorer. It discovers the Van Allen radiation belt, which causes the polar lights called Aurora Borealis (in the Northern Hemisphere) and Aurora Australis (in the Southern Hemisphere).

▶ The Aurora Borealis photographed over Norway

12 April, 1961

The Soviets manage another first by launching the cosmonaut Yuri Gagarin into space.

◀ *Yuri Gagarin, the first man in space and the first to orbit Earth*

25 May, 1961

US President John F Kennedy publicly commits the US to achieving the first human landing on the Moon.

◀ *US President John F Kennedy addressing Congress in 1961, announcing his ambitious goal of "landing a man on the Moon and returning him safely to Earth"*

16 June, 1963

The Soviet Union launches Vostok-6 with Valentina Tereshkova, the first female cosmonaut to travel to outer space.

◀ *The first woman in space, Valentina Tereshkova, presenting a badge to the first man on the Moon, Neil Armstrong*

20 February, 1962

NASA's 'human computers', an all-woman team of mathematicians, undertake mind-boggling calculations that give the US an edge in the space race. Katherine G Johnson's impressive mathematics skills help put American astronaut John Glenn into orbit around Earth.

◀ *Katherine G Johnson, whose calculations in orbital mechanics led to many successful missions, including the first Moon landing*

▲ *This USSR stamp from 1965 commemorates Leonov's historic walk in space*

28 November, 1964

The Mariner-4 explorer is launched. It becomes the first spacecraft to fly by Mars and send photographs and data about the planet.

18 March, 1965

The Soviet cosmonaut Alexei Leonov becomes the first man to 'walk' in space. He leaves the spacecraft wearing an early spacesuit and walks in the vacuum of space for just over 12 minutes.

20 July, 1969

After a series of missions under the Apollo programme, the US spacecraft Apollo-11 lands on the Moon. Crew members Neil Armstrong and Buzz Aldrin spend 21 hours and 30 minutes on the Moon before successfully returning to the spacecraft. This brilliant achievement marks the end of the Cold War space race.

◀ *Buzz Aldrin on the Moon; reflected in his visor is Neil Armstrong taking the photograph*

Kicking off Space Exploration

Scientists have been working on fulfilling the human dream of space travel for centuries. During 1642–1727, Isaac Newton published his laws of motion and described gravity. This gave us a scientific basis for understanding rockets and orbits. Russian scientist Konstantin Tsiolkovsky (1857–1935) showed how rockets could be used to launch spacecrafts. He also calculated the minimum speed required to stay in orbit around Earth. Finally, in 1942, the German aerospace engineer Werner von Braun and his team built V2, the first rocket to reach the boundaries of space, about 100 kilometres above Earth.

🔍 Rocket Development

A rocket is any weapon or vehicle propelled by a rocket engine. The medieval Chinese inventors of rockets used gunpowder for propulsion. Liquid-fuel rockets were developed by Robert H Goddard (1882–1945), the father of modern rocketry.

Modern ion rockets use solar-powered electricity to produce a stream of **ions**, which propel the rocket forward. The latest **plasma** rockets use radio waves to heat chemicals to such a high temperature that they turn to plasma (which is what the Sun is made of)! A powerful rocket like this could travel to Mars and back within a few weeks. But scientists have yet to figure out how to stop the rocket from melting in the heat it generates.

▼ US officials, including Werner von Braun, with a model Explorer-1, the first satellite launched by the US into outer space.

👤✓ In Real Life

Many space exploration devices are launched on multi-stage rockets. These are made of two to five rockets, each of which carries its own engine and fuel.

▼ The evolution of Soviet space launch vehicles from the R-7 (the first-ever Intercontinental Ballistic Missile), the Sputnik launcher, the Vostok, the Voskhod launcher and the Soyuz launcher

▶ India's PSLV, a four-stage launch vehicle with both solid-fuel and liquid-fuel rockets

R-7 (8K71)
Test vehicle
1957

8K71PS Sputnik
(PS) Launcher
1957

8 K72K Vostok
(3KA) Launcher
1960

11A57 Voskhod
(3KV) Launcher
1963

11A57 Soyuz
(7K-OK) Launcher
1966

Sputnik

Launched on an R-7 liquid-fuel rocket, the Soviet Union's Sputnik was the first artificial satellite to orbit Earth. It weighed 83.6 kilograms and travelled in an elliptical path above Earth for three months. At 29,000 kmph, it took 96.2 minutes to complete each orbit. After 1440 circuits, it burned up in Earth's atmosphere on 4 January, 1958.

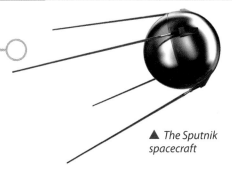

▲ *The Sputnik spacecraft*

A Cosmic Zoo

The first beings to go up in a rocket were most likely accidental passengers like bacteria or other microbes. In 1947, scientists sent up some fruit flies in a V2 rocket. They were given some corn to snack on during the trip. On 14 June, 1949, Albert II became the first monkey to fly up in a rocket. He travelled 134 kilometres to the very beginning of space. Since then, 32 monkeys and a chimpanzee have journeyed to space. Several mice were launched during the 1950s. The dog Laika was the first animal to orbit Earth. Sputnik-5 was the first spacecraft to return with its passengers alive on 19 August, 1960. These included 2 dogs, a rabbit, 42 mice, 2 rats and fruit flies!

▲ *After some confused attempts, Arabella became the first spider to spin a web in space. Launched in 1972, Arabella and Anita were the first spiders in outer space*

◀ *The US launch of the V2 rocket carrying Albert II*

The First Spaceman

Flying the rocket Vostok-1, Yuri Gagarin (1934–1968) became the first man in outer space. From there, he launched into orbit on the Vostok 3KA spacecraft and successfully orbited Earth. He famously whistled the tune of 'The Motherland hears, the Motherland knows, Where her son flies in the sky', a 1951 song by Dmitri Shostakovich. Awed by the sight before him, he reported to ground control, "The Earth is blue... How wonderful. It is amazing."

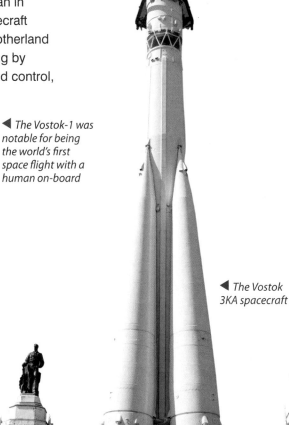

◀ *The Vostok-1 was notable for being the world's first space flight with a human on-board*

◀ *The Vostok 3KA spacecraft*

To the Moon and Back

In 1961, President John F Kennedy announced that the US would put men on the Moon before 1970. NASA achieved this goal when, on 20 July, 1969, the manned Apollo-11 spacecraft made a successful landing. Nearly 530 million people watched the event on live broadcast. Since then, there have been several missions to the Moon launched by the US, Russia, Japan, China, India and Europe.

▶ *From left to right, this shows the Moon's near side, far side, north pole and south pole*

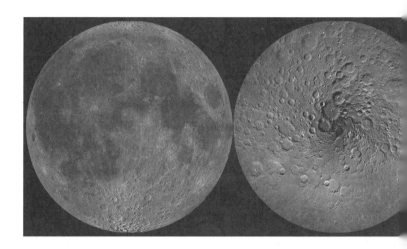

💡 Isn't It Amazing!

Just between the mid-60s and the mid-70s, there were some 65 Moon landings! However, only 6 Moon landings have carried human beings on board and only 12 people have ever walked on the Moon's cratered surface.

◀ *On 30 May, 1966, the US robot spaceship Surveyor-1 reached the Moon. Its photographs gave NASA vital information on how they might successfully land a crew of astronauts on the satellite*

🔍 The Dark Side of the Moon

The first human beings to orbit the Moon were the crew of the Apollo-8. It comprised Frank Borman, James Lovell and William Anders. The event occurred on 24 December, 1968. While orbiting the Moon, they also became the first people ever to see the dark side of the Earth's Moon.

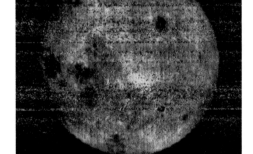

▶ *William Anders's photo of Earth rising over the Moon's horizon, taken from Apollo-8, is one of the most iconic photographs in human history*

◀ *Our first view of the far side of the Moon came from a photograph taken by Soviet probe Luna-3 on 7 October, 1959*

🔍 Man on the Moon

Apollo-11 launched on 16 July, 1969. It carried Neil Armstrong, Michael Collins and Edwin 'Buzz' Aldrin. On 20 July, Armstrong and Aldrin donned their spacesuits and climbed into a lunar landing module called Eagle, while Collins remained in orbit in the Columbia module.

The Eagle landed on a volcanic plain called Mare Tranquillity. Armstrong and Aldrin spent 21 hours and 36 minutes resting, exploring and deploying experiments. They then re-joined Collins. On 24 July, Apollo-11 splashed down in the Pacific Ocean and the three astronauts were safely brought back home.

◄ The Apollo-11 lunar crew (from left to right): Neil Armstrong, Michael Collins and Buzz Aldrin

▶ The Eagle with its spidery landing pods and sensors, photographed in orbit by Columbia

▶ Apollo-11 lifting off on the three-stage, liquid-fuelled Saturn V rocket on 16 July, 1969 from Kennedy Space Centre

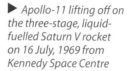

🔍 The Miraculous Apollo-13

Apollo-13 was meant to be the third manned mission to land on the Moon. But two days into its journey, it experienced an explosion due to faulty wiring. The astronauts seemed doomed. Fortunately, NASA's scientists found a solution using the limited equipment on board. They guided the astronauts to make the repairs and brought them home safely. The heroic story is celebrated in books, films, theatre and even comics!

🔍 Lunar Road Trips

From 1971 onwards, American astronauts used a Moon car to explore the vast surface of Earth's satellite. This electric-powered vehicle, with a top speed of less than 13 kmph, was called the Lunar Rover. The Moon buggy made its first trip on 31 July, 1971 with Apollo-15 astronauts David Scott and James Irwin.

🔍 Modern Explorations

Since the 1990s, Japan's Institute of Space and Aeronautical Sciences, the European Space Agency, the Chinese Lunar Exploration Agency and the Indian Space Research Organisation have all successfully sent missions to the Moon. The first private enterprise to do so was the Manfred Memorial Moon Mission (4M), launched on 23 October, 2014. On 3 January, 2019, China's Chang'e 4 (named after the Moon goddess) became the first mission to achieve a soft landing directly on the far side of the Moon!

👤 In Real Life

Neil Armstrong's words "One small step for man, one giant leap for mankind" were not the first words said on the Moon. In reality, the first words were a practical post-landing checklist! Armstrong's first communication from the Moon was simply, "Houston, Tranquillity Base here. The Eagle has landed."

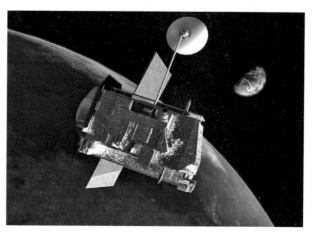

▲ The Lunar Reconnaissance Orbiter orbiting the Moon and mapping its polar regions

Space Missions: Inner Planets

While the US was planning its many missions to the Moon, the Soviet Union was aiming for other planets. On 12 February, 1961, Venera-1 became the first probe launched to another planet—Venus. Though the probe failed, the Venera series made steady progress. On 18 October, 1967, a capsule from Venera-4 entered Venus's atmosphere and successfully took direct measurements. Great leaps have since been made in the exploration of the Inner Planets and of the asteroid belt on the group's outer boundary.

◀ *Launched by the US on 27 August, 1962 on the Atlas Agena B rocket, Mariner-2 was the first space probe to fly by Venus and record the planet's temperature and atmospheric data*

Mercury

The least explored of the Inner Planets, Mercury has been visited only by the Mariner-10 and the MESSENGER. The Mariner-10 photographed about 45 per cent of Mercury over 1974–1975, while orbiting the Sun. The MESSENGER flew by Mercury three times in 2008–2009. It entered the planet's orbit in 2011, mapped it completely and continued to collect data till 30 April, 2015. The latest mission to Mercury, the BepiColombo, was launched jointly by Europe and Japan in late 2018. It is expected to achieve its first flight by the planet in 2021 and stay in orbit till 2028.

▲ *This false-colour image of Mercury taken by MESSENGER shows cliff-like landforms that look like stairs. These geologically young features mean that the planet is still contracting and, like Earth, is tectonically active*

Venus

Many spacecrafts have visited Venus, most notably the Soviet Union's Venera series. In 1969, Venera 5 and 6 were the first to deploy multiple instruments and **landers** into Venus's atmosphere. On 27 March, 1972, Venera-8 successfully landed on Venus's surface. Japan's Akatsuki (meaning Dawn) space probe is currently in orbit, studying the planet's atmosphere and gravity.

◀ *A radar image of Venus within the clouds, taken by NASA's Magellan on 29 October, 1991*

▲ *A photo of Venus, taken by NASA's Mariner-10, shows a planet hidden under thick sulphuric clouds*

Mars

Mars has been the destination of several orbiters, landers and rovers since the 1960s. Launched in 2001, NASA's Mars Odyssey orbiter is the longest-serving spacecraft around Mars. It will most likely remain there till 2025. More recently, the Indian Space Research Organisation (ISRO) put its Mars Orbiter Mission into orbit on 24 September, 2014. It is the fourth space agency to reach Mars after USSR, USA and Europe. India is also the only country to have achieved success in its first attempt.

◀ *On 2 December, 1971, Mars-3 became the first spacecraft to soft-land an instrument-bearing pod on the planet. At the time, there was a planet-wide dust storm and the pod could send back data for only 20 seconds*

Mars Rover

On 4 July, 1997, the US lander called Mars Pathfinder sent out a robotic motor vehicle called Sojourner to explore the surface of Mars. This was the first Mars rover. In January, 2004, the twin rovers Spirit and Opportunity also landed on Mars. They reported great discoveries such as the presence of liquid water in the planet's past. The largest, fastest and most advanced rover yet is Curiosity, which joined the twins on 6 August, 2012.

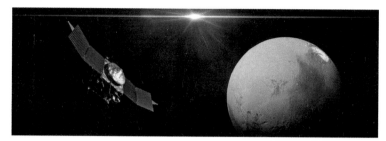

▲ NASA's latest spacecraft, MAVEN, near Mars. The planet can be seen with its northern ice cap, Planum Boreum. Its southern polar cap is called Planum Australe

Isn't It Amazing!

Martian windstorms and dust devils actually cleaned the twin rovers' solar panels, which increased their lifespan!

The Asteroid Belt

Asteroids are airless rocks that orbit the Sun. They mainly lie in a belt just beyond Mars. The largest object in the asteroid belt is Ceres. It was discovered in 1801 by astronomer Giuseppe Piazzi. There are now 7,81,692 known asteroids and we are still counting. Launched on 17 February, 1996, NEAR Shoemaker was the first dedicated asteroid probe. It photographed 253 Mathilde in 1997 and landed on 433 Eros in 2001. In 2010, the Japanese Hayabusa became the first probe to send back asteroid samples.

	21 Lutetia
	253 Mathilde
	243 Ida (243) Ida I Dactyl
	433 Eros
	951 Gaspra
	2867 Šteins
4 Vesta	25143 Itokawa

▲ A representation of the comparative sizes of eight asteroids

▼ The rover Opportunity in a Martian crater

Space Missions: Outer Planets

The Outer Planets of our solar system lie beyond the asteroid belt. They are Jupiter, Saturn, Uranus and Neptune. Beyond Neptune is the Kuiper Belt, a region of icy rocks and dwarf planets like Pluto. Even beyond this, forming the boundary of the solar system is the mysterious Oort Cloud, a collection of comets and unexplored matter. While Jupiter's atmosphere has been explored by a handful of spacecrafts, only four missions have been to Saturn and just one to each of the planets farther away.

▲ In 1995, NASA's Galileo became the first spacecraft to orbit Jupiter. It captured these clear images of Jupiter's four largest moons—Io, Europa, Ganymede and Callisto

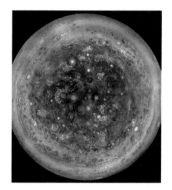

▲ Since 2016, the space probe Juno has been keeping an eye on Jupiter, sending photos such as this image of a storm on the planet's south pole in 2017

🔍 The Pioneer Programme

Beginning in 1958, the US sent a series of unmanned space missions under its Pioneer programme. The earliest of these missions were simply attempts to leave Earth. The greatest successes of the programme came with the launch of Pioneer 10 and 11 in the 1970s. Both explored the Outer Planets and left the solar system.

🔍 Pioneer-10

Launched on 2 March, 1972, Pioneer-10 became the first spacecraft to go beyond the asteroid belt. It began photographing Jupiter in November 1973 and sent back some 500 images.

Its instruments gathered groundbreaking data on the planet's environment. Pioneer-10 then became the first man-made object to gather enough velocity (**escape velocity**) to leave the solar system. Its last, weak radio signal was received on 23 January, 2003, when the probe was 12 billion kilometres away.

💡 Isn't It Amazing!

Just in case they meet extra-terrestrial intelligence someday, Pioneer 10 and 11 carry a plaque with information about Earth and drawings of a man and a woman.

▶ The plaque aboard Pioneer 10 and 11

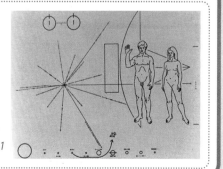

▲ The 258-kilogram Pioneer-10 under construction

🔍 The Voyagers

Launched in 1977, the robotic probes Voyager 1 and 2 aimed to study the outer solar system. Over these 40-plus years, they have made a string of grand discoveries such as active volcanoes on Io, a possible ocean underneath the icy crust of Europa, methane clouds and rain on Titan, Neptune's Great Dark Spot and geysers in the polar cap of Triton (Neptune's moon).

In August 2002, Voyager-1 became the first spacecraft to leave the **heliosphere** and enter **interstellar space**. Voyager-2 is the only spacecraft to have visited Uranus and Neptune. It followed Voyager-1 into interstellar space in November 2018. Both probes are still sending back information through the Deep Space Network *(see pp 16–17)*

▲ *The eruption of volcano Loki on Jupiter's moon Io was captured on film by Voyager-1*

◄ *Voyager-2's photos of Neptune from 1989 show its storms—the Great Dark Spot, the bright white Scooter just below it and Dark Spot 2 (farther down) with its bright centre*

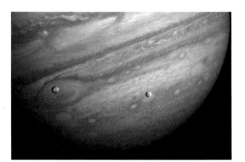
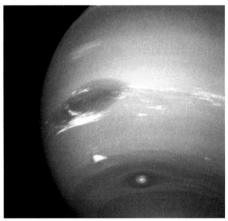

▲ *Voyager–1 took this photo of Io and Europa on 13 February, 1979. Io is about 3,50,000 kilometres above Jupiter's Great Red Spot; Europa is about 6,00,000 kilometres above Jupiter's clouds*

🔍 Cassini-Huygens

Launched on 15 October, 1997, Cassini-Huygens is a joint mission between NASA, ESA and the Italian Space Agency to study Saturn, its rings and its moons. The main probe, NASA's Cassini, was active for almost 20 years, photographing Venus, Earth, the asteroid 2685 Masursky, Jupiter and, of course, Saturn and its environs. Also, on board is the ESA's Huygens lander, which landed on Titan, Saturn's largest moon. The mission was a huge success and even gave scientists an idea of where else we might find life in the solar system.

▶ *In March 2012, Cassini photographed a huge storm churning through Saturn's atmosphere*

🔍 New Horizons

Launched in 2006 as part of NASA's New Frontiers programme, New Horizons explored Pluto in 2015 and is now heading towards the Kuiper belt objects.

👤 In Real Life

Launched on 5 April, 1973, Pioneer-11 became the first craft to make direct observations of Saturn.

▶ *This image of Pluto, taken in 2015 by New Horizons, shows its icy 'heart' of nitrogen and methane*

Artificial Satellites

The idea of putting a man-made object into orbit around Earth was proposed as early as 1928. Slovenian rocket engineer Herman Potocnik (1892–1929) described how we could communicate with such a satellite using radio signals. He also described a space station and its usefulness in Earth-related experiments. Since then, human beings have developed many kinds of satellites. There are close to 2,000 satellites around our planet. Inventors have also created sophisticated networking systems to communicate with them.

▶ An Advanced Extremely High Frequency (AEHF) communications satellite

Deep Space Network

The awe-inspiring Deep Space Network (DSN) is an array of giant radio antennae located in three far-flung places—California, USA; near Madrid, Spain; and near Canberra, Australia. This careful placement allows DSN to remain in continuous contact with spacecrafts, even as our planet keeps rotating. The DSN guides spacecrafts and probes that are travelling far in space. It also receives information and photographs from these unmanned explorers. Furthermore, DSN communicates with some satellites orbiting Earth and studies celestial objects using radio frequencies.

Building a Satellite

These days, a satellite is designed to be strong and as light as possible. It is made of a platform (called bus) which contains the main systems. This includes batteries, computers and engine thrusters. The antennae, solar cells and instruments for research and communication are attached to the bus. The solar cells are usually designed on to foldable wings that are many metres long. Satellites are also covered with blankets of aluminium foil that can protect it from extreme heat and cold.

▲ The Deep Space Network operations room in California, USA

▶ Miniature satellites, such as this Estonian CubeSat, weigh less than 500 kilograms and serve many purposes, including data gathering and signal relay

▼ The giant parabolic antennae of the DSN are located in a bowl-shaped area created by hills to increase the antennae's sensitivity to specific radio signals

🔍 Finding the Way

The Global Positioning System (GPS) in your car, which tells you how to get from one place to another, functions because of navigation satellites. These are the same satellites that guide ships, aircrafts and many other important systems. Navigation satellite systems that offer global coverage are called Global Navigation Satellite Systems (GNSS). The USA's GPS and Russia's GLONASS are two powerful examples of GNSS.

▶ *The highly precise and detailed maps that show you the way while you drive use time signals from navigation satellites*

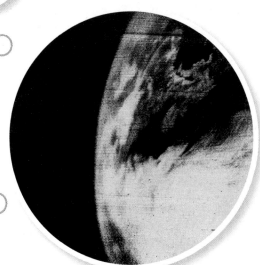

🔍 Communication & Entertainment

Our TVs, phones, radios and Internet all work on light signals or electromagnetic waves transmitted by communication satellites. Since these signals can only travel in straight lines, multiple satellites work together to transmit signals around the globe. Active satellites receive signals from a source, amplify it and redirect it to the receiver. Passive satellites simply receive and redirect a signal.

🔍 Monitoring the Weather

About 36,000 kilometres above us are geostationary satellites that track weather patterns and changes. **Geostationary** means that the satellite keeps up with Earth's spin, so it is always looking down on us from the same spot. The polar satellite is another kind of weather satellite. It orbits at right angles to the equator—about 800 kilometres above us—and passes around the North Pole and South Pole.

▲ *The first television image of Earth taken from TIROS-1, the first successful weather satellite*

🔍 Planet Observation

Earth observation satellites detect changes in our planet's green cover, ocean surfaces and radiation. They also map Earth. Along with communications satellites, they are used by military and spy agencies to collect information that is of national importance. When used for such a purpose, they are called reconnaissance satellites.

▼ *The A-Train constellation of 2014 refers to seven Earth-observation satellites, though some of them are no longer an active part of the system*

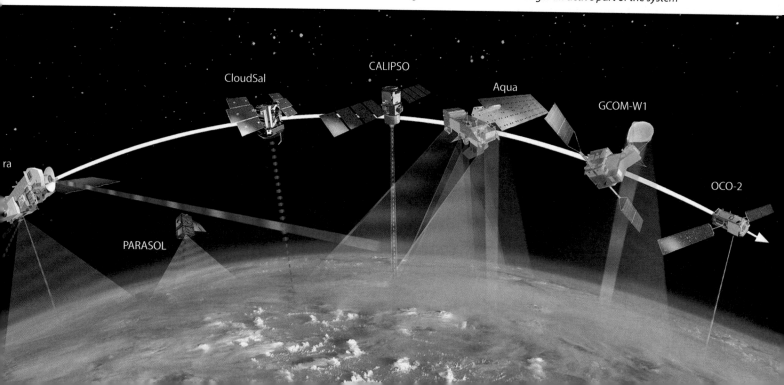

Galaxy, Intelsat and Television

Galaxy is the name given to a series of over 30 communications satellites. They are owned and operated by the Intelsat Corporation. On 6 April, 1965, Intelsat-1 (also known as Early Bird) became the first commercial communications satellite. Launched on 28 June, 1983, Galaxy-1 was among the earliest geostationary satellites. Intelsat's network of satellites showed us worldwide events like the Olympic Games. Even the hotline that connects the White House (USA) and the Kremlin (Russia) is linked over Intelsat's satellites.

◀ The Intelsat–IVA communications satellite under construction in the 1970s

Navstar GPS

The US government's satellite-based navigation system is called Navstar GPS. Its first satellite, Block-I, was launched in 1978. Nine more followed soon. Over 1989–1994, a new series of 24 Block-II satellites were sent up to complete the GPS system. Each satellite weighs about 900 kilograms and has 17-metre-long solar panels. The key GPS parts are 12 helical antennae and one spear-like antenna; they send and receive signals.

In Real Life

The first public satellite TV signals sent from America to millions of TVs in England and France were relayed over the Telstar satellite on 23 July, 1962.

Incredible Individuals

British science fiction writer Arthur C Clarke is often called the inventor of communications satellites. In 1945, he proposed a global communications system that worked using three satellites spaced equally apart while orbiting Earth.

◀ Arthur C Clarke on the sets of the epic science fiction film 2001: A Space Odyssey

Misty the Spy

Key Hole (KH) refers to a series of US reconnaissance satellites. The latest KH-13 is also known as Misty, an Enhanced Imaging System that was launched in the late 90s. It is said to be about 18,143.7 kilograms in weight, but the mission is so confidential that such details cannot be confirmed. Even the satellite's name keeps changing! Misty is thought to be spying by taking photographs, but the subjects of these photographs remain a tightly guarded secret.

▼ Declassified in 2011, the KH-9 reconnaissance satellite—codenamed HEXAGON and commonly known as Big Bird—was exhibited to the public for a single day

◀ A depiction of the Block-II Navstar GPS satellite

TERRA Observes Earth

Launched on 18 December, 1999, the TERRA polar orbiter is the flagship satellite of NASA's Earth Observing System. The size of a small bus, TERRA travels from North Pole to South Pole once every 99 minutes. On 6 October, 2018, it completed 1,00,000 orbits. Terra carries five instruments that measure Earth's atmosphere, ocean, land, snow and ice, and energy budget. These are called ASTER, CERES, MISR, MOPITT and MODIS.

▲ *TERRA photographed the horrific Deepwater Horizon oil spill on 30 April, 2010. When seen from space, this spill appears in the shape of two interlocking commas. It is one of the largest marine oil-slicks in human history*

▶ *GOES-13 satellite travelling to space on the Delta–IV rocket*

GOES, NOAA and Weather Monitoring

The National Oceanic and Atmospheric Administration (NOAA) is a US agency that monitors the atmosphere and water bodies of Earth. Its geostationary GOES series of satellites focus on distinct parts of the planet, watching for atmospheric changes that lead to storms, tornadoes, flash floods and hurricanes. NOAA also has a series of polar satellites that spin around the globe, spotting developing climatic catastrophes.

LANDSAT: Recording Human Impact on Earth

Launched on 23 July, 1972, the Earth Resources Technology satellite was eventually renamed LANDSAT. The programme has since sent up seven more satellites to take millions of images of the planet. The record now shows significant global changes in farmlands, forests and urban and suburban spreads. The images are studied by map-makers and used extensively by educators as well. LANDSAT is now the longest-running programme on Earth observation.

▶ *LANDSAT 7 was launched in 1999*

Space Agencies

There are currently 72 government-run space agencies in the world. Private agencies like SpaceX are also making progress in this conquest.

🔍 China National Space Administration (CNSA)

China's space programme began in the 1950s with the ex-NASA talent Qian Xuesen. The CNSA itself was established in 1993. In 2003, China became the third country in the world to send a man to space. In 2019, the Chang'e 4 achieved the first soft landing on the dark side of the Moon!

◀ *Yang Liwei became China's first taikonaut (Chinese astronaut) when he travelled to space on the Shenzou-5 on 15 October, 2003*

🔍 European Space Agency (ESA)

An organisation of 22 countries, the ESA was established in 1975. It has paved the way for unified and peaceful developments in space.

ESA also runs Envisat, the world's largest, most complex environmental satellite.

◀ *ESA's Artemis is Europe's most advanced telecommunications satellite*

🔍 Roscosmos

Roscosmos handles the cosmonautics programmes for Russia. Some of its most interesting research involves sending up geckos, silkworm eggs, seeds, fruit flies, mushrooms and other life forms to study space biology.

🔍 Japan Aerospace Exploration Agency (JAXA)

Japan's space exploration began in the mid-1950s, led by the brilliant Hideo Itokawa. JAXA was formed on 1 October, 2003. It handles technological development and advanced missions like exploring asteroids. JAXA is the first agency to obtain asteroid samples through a successful return mission.

▶ *Tanegashima Space Center launching JAXA's H-IIA rocket with the lunar orbit explorer Kaguya*

🔍 National Aeronautics and Space Administration (NASA)

The USA's space research and missions are handled by NASA, which explores the universe through robots and satellites. NASA furthers Earth and Sun research through its Earth Observing System and the Heliophysics Research Program.

▲ *NASA astronaut Ed White performing the first US spacewalk on Gemini-4*

🔍 Indian Space Research Organisation (ISRO)

India's space programme was founded by the scientist Vikram Sarabhai. ISRO itself was formed in 1969. Its first satellite, Aryabhata, was launched in 1975. ISRO's 2014 Mars Orbiter Mission made India the first nation to reach the planet in its first attempt! In 2017, ISRO launched a record 104 satellites on a single rocket.

Telescopes: A Distant Look

Space scientists these days have incredibly powerful telescopes locked on to far-off galaxies and planets. They even have telescopes in space. These astronomical satellites study the cosmos without suffering from any atmospheric disturbances. The idea of space telescopes came from physicist Lyman Spitzer in 1946. The first successful one, the OAO-2, was launched by the US in 1968.

▼ *The Hubble Space Telescope*

Space Telescopes

NASA's 'Great Observatories' refers to four powerful space telescopes. The Compton Gamma Ray Observatory observes **gamma rays** in space, the Chandra Observatory observes **X-rays**, the Spitzer Space Telescope observes **infrared rays** and the Hubble Space Telescope observes visible light.

◀ *Images from Chandra, Hubble and Spitzer combined show the Crab Nebula spewing energy at the rate of 1,00,000 Suns*

Gemini Observatory

Famous for its twin 8.1-metre diameter telescopes, the Gemini Observatory is located in the mountains of Hawaii and Chile. From here, Gemini's telescopes are able to keep the entire sky under scrutiny.

European Southern Observatory (ESO)

Created in 1962, ESO observes the skies from three sites in the Atacama Desert, Chile—La Silla, Paranal and Chajnantor. With its 3.5-metre New Technology Telescope, ESO invented the method of using computers to control telescopes' mirrors. ESO also runs the Very Large Telescope (VLT), which discovered the first **exoplanet**. The VLT is currently observing stars that are close to the supermassive black hole at the centre of our galaxy.

WM Keck Observatory

The two-telescope WM Keck Observatory lies 4,145 metres high, near the peak of old volcano Mauna Kea, in Hawaii. With their 10-metre primary mirrors, these telescopes are among the largest astronomical telescopes in the world. They are responsible for achievements such as discovering the existence of galaxies at the edge of the universe and studying supernovas to find out how fast the universe is expanding.

▶ *Located at the Roque de los Muchachos Observatory in the Canaries, Spain, the 10.4-metre Gran Telescopio Canarias is the largest single-aperture optical telescope in the world*

💡 Isn't It Amazing!

The ESO 3.6-metre telescope uses an instrument called HARPS, which has discovered 130 extrasolar planets till date!

▲ *Located 2400 metres high in the mountains of the Atacama Desert, La Silla has several sophisticated optical telescopes pointed at the sky*

Bright-tailed Comets

Comets are small bodies of frozen gas, rock and dust orbiting the Sun. They are leftover material from the formation of our solar system about 4.6 billion years ago. When a comet comes closer to the Sun, its dust and gas start to heat up and escape. This gives the comet a glowing head and a tail that can stretch for millions of miles!

◄ *The comet is made of the nucleus (the solid, stable part), the coma (a dense cloud of water and gases), the dust tail (made of millions of kilometres of smoke-sized particles) and the ion tail (composed of several hundred million kilometres of plasma and ions)*

◄ *The long-period comet Hale-Bopp was so bright and large, it was called the Great Comet of 1997. It was discovered on 23 July, 1995, independently by both Alan Hale and Thomas Bopp*

🏅 Incredible Individuals

Comets were discovered in ancient times. Most notably, Halley's Comet first appeared in Chinese records of c. 240 BCE. It appeared again in the beautiful Bayeux Tapestry that depicts the conquest of England in 1066.

▲ *The star of Bethlehem in Giotto's mesmerising Adoration of the Magi (c.1305) is said to be inspired by Halley's Comet, spotted four years before the date of this painting*

🔍 Where do Comets come From?

In 1951, astronomer Gerard Kuiper correctly proposed that comets come from a belt of icy bodies beyond Neptune. The force of the Sun's gravity draws some of these objects inwards into a closer orbit. These are called short-period comets. They take less than 200 years to complete a single orbit of the Sun. Long-period comets arrive from a region even beyond the Kuiper belt. This mysterious region at the edge of our solar system is called the Oort Cloud. The comets here can take up to 30 million years to complete their orbit!

Halley's Comet

The short-period Halley's Comet can be seen by the naked eye as it comes close to the Sun. This last occurred in 1986 and will happen again in 2061. It is named after English astronomer Edmond Halley, who first predicted the comet's periodic occurrence. During the 1986 appearance, several probes were launched to study the comet more closely. Photos from the Soviet Vega-1 started coming in on 4 March, 1986. These included the first-ever image of its nucleus. Others that successfully studied the comet are Vega 2, the ESA's Giotto, and the two Japanese probes Suisei and Sakigake. Together, they are all known as the Halley Armada.

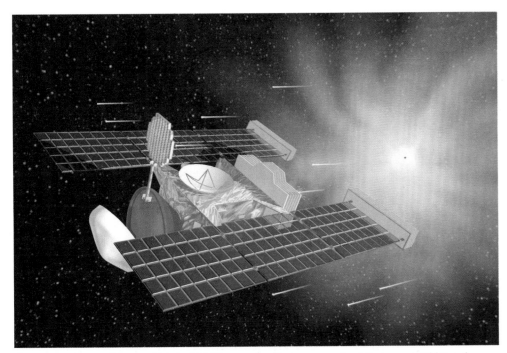

▲ Launched on 7 February, 1999, the 390-kilogram Stardust space probe visited comet Wild-2 and brought back the first samples of comet dust on 15 January, 2006

◄ On 4 July, 2005, NASA's Deep Impact space probe successfully sent an impactor to collide with the comet Tempel-1 (resulting in a bright flare) to study questions on impact craters and comet composition

Rosetta Probe

The ESA's Rosetta space probe was launched on 2 March, 2004 to study the comet 67P/Churyumov–Gerasimenko. It reached the comet on 6 August, 2014 and settled into orbit within 10–30 kilometres of the body. On 12 November, Rosetta sent out its lander module Philae, which made the first successful landing on a comet. The probe was thus able to make detailed studies, rendering the mission a triumph for the agency.

▲ Rosetta's photo of comet Churyumov–Gerasimenko

Jean-Louis Pons (1761–1831), a self-taught French astronomer, discovered a record 37 comets over 1801–1827. The other prolific discoverer of comets was British-born American William Robert Brooks (1844–1921).

Caroline Herschel (1750–1848), a lauded German astronomer, was the first woman to discover a series of comets.

Gottfried Kirch (1639–1710) made the first telescopic discovery of a comet—the Komet C/1680 V1, also called Kirch's Comet.

Edward Emerson Barnard (1857–1923) was the first to discover a comet through photographic methods. This was comet 206P/Barnard-Boattini, on the night of 13 October, 1892.

Incidents and Accidents

Human exploration of space has been an odyssey of hair-raising exploits and tragic misadventures. We owe a great deal to our heroic space pioneers. Each small step of their cosmic tussle has led to giant leaps in our understanding of the universe.

23 March, 1961

The first space-related fatality occurs during a low-pressure endurance experiment. A Soviet fighter pilot and trainee cosmonaut drops an alcohol-soaked cloth on a hotplate. Extra oxygen in the chamber (50 per cent, compared to the 21 per cent in normal air) leads to a fire, killing Valentin Bondarenko.

17 May, 1930

Austrian rocketry pioneer Max Valier dies in a rocket-engine explosion in Berlin, becoming the tragic first casualty of the modern space age.

▲ *Valier in a rocket car*

18 March, 1965

Alexei Leonov's famous first spacewalk nearly ends in disaster when his spacesuit inflates while he is still in the vacuum of space. It becomes so big, he is unable to re-enter the spacecraft. He is able to open a valve and let off some of the pressure from the suit.

▲ *Leonov's spacesuit*

Leonov's spacesuit deflates just enough for him to re-enter the capsule. The spacecraft becomes so cramped, the crew's landing gets affected. They end up in a deep forest and spend a frigid couple of nights in makeshift huts, before a helicopter flies to their rescue.

24 April, 1967

The first in-flight tragedy in the history of the space age affects Soyuz-1. Its sole crewman, Colonel Vladimir Komarov dies after the craft's parachutes fail to open during descent and the capsule crashes into the ground.

⊛ Incredible Individuals

During the Apollo-14 mission of 1971, the American astronaut Alan Shepard became the first and only person to hit golf balls on the Moon. The balls are still up there!

▲ *Alexei Leonov*

14 November, 1969

Apollo-12 becomes the sixth manned mission to the Moon. During its launch, it is struck by lightning twice! The crew spends extra time in orbit ensuring that there is no damage that will affect their mission to the Moon.

▲ The 'Fallen Astronaut' is a small sculpture on the Moon which, along with a commemorative plaque, honours pioneering cosmonauts such as Komarov

7 February, 1984

Astronauts often tether themselves to a spacecraft while walking out in space. Bruce McCandless achieves the first untethered spacewalk on Challenger mission STS-41-B.

◀ McCandless on his famous untethered spacewalk

25 July, 1984

During the Soyuz T-12 mission, Svetlana Savitskaya becomes the first woman to take a spacewalk.

28 January, 1986

The Space Shuttle Challenger disintegrates 73 seconds into its lift-off. Cold weather causes one of its seals to fail, which in turn lets in hot gases from the rocket and leads to the disaster. The tragedy claims the lives of all seven crew members.

▲ The Challenger explosion

17 June, 1985

Royal Saudi Air Force pilot Sultan bin Salman bin Abdulaziz Al Saud becomes the first member of royalty to fly to outer space. He still holds the record for being the youngest person to fly on the Space Shuttle, at the age of 28.

◀ Al Saud on his NASA mission

11 March, 2001

Susan J Helms and James S Voss set the record for the longest time spent outside a space vehicle at 8 hours and 56 minutes.

▲ Helms viewing Earth from a window on the ISS

1 February, 2003

Space Shuttle Columbia's left wing fails while re-entering the atmosphere after a two-week mission. The entire capsule breaks apart 65 kilometres above Earth and falls in fragments over Texas and Louisiana, USA. All seven crew members lose their lives.

▶ Remembering the crew of Columbia: (from left) mission specialist David Brown, commander Rick Husband, mission specialist Laurel Clark, mission specialist Kalpana Chawla, mission specialist Michael Anderson, pilot William McCool and Israeli payload specialist Ilan Ramon

Space Stations

Certain artificial satellites stay in low Earth orbit and people can live inside them. These are called space stations. The earliest such station was Salyut-1, launched by the Soviet Union on 19 April, 1971. It was built as one complete piece and sent up to space; the crew followed afterwards. Space stations have come a long way since then.

◀ *A 1971 stamp commemorating Salyut-1 and its three brave astronauts*

🔍 The Salyut Programme

Over 1971–1986, the Soviet Union explored the possibility of living in space. They called the mission Salyut. Over these 15 years, they successfully sent up four space stations for scientific research and two for military purposes. All six had human crew members. Of course, there were failures too. Two other Salyut launches failed. The world's first manned mission to a space station, Salyut-1, ended in grief when the crew died just before re-entry to Earth. On 30 June, 1971, a pressure valve on the descending Soyuz-11 opened too early, suffocating the three astronauts.

💡 Isn't It Amazing!

During its launch, Skylab hit a micro-meteoroid. The impact deprived the craft of electricity and thermal protection! Fortunately, the crew was able to repair Skylab. It was the first time such a large repair was conducted in space.

▶ *Astronauts building part of a space station as it orbits Earth*

▲ *The International Space Station with its vast array of solar panels*

Skylab

Skylab, NASA's first space station, was inhabited for some 24 weeks over 1973–1974. It bore a solar observatory (Apollo Telescope Mount), two docking ports, EVA capabilities and a main working area called Orbital Workshop. Skylab teams made breakthrough progress in solar science and Earth observation. They also broke Salyut's record of longest stay in space, taking it from 23 days to 84 days.

Mir

The first space station to be put together in space was the Soviet Union's Mir. The core unit and modules (with specific functions) were launched separately and assembled in orbit over 1986–1996. This became the standard way of building space stations. Mir was continuously inhabited for 3644 days. It still holds the record for the longest single human space flight. Over 1994–1995, astronaut Valeriy Polyakov spent 437 days and 18 hours on the space station.

The International Space Station (ISS)

The ISS is the biggest man-made object that has ever flown in space. It orbits Earth 16 times a day. Five space agencies came together to create the ISS—NASA, Roscosmos, JAXA, ESA and CSA (Canada). Its first component, Zarya was launched in 1998. Its first permanent crew arrived on Expedition-1 on 2 November, 2000. ISS has since been occupied continuously for over 19 years! The space station has been visited by cosmonauts and even tourists from 18 nations.

▶ A view of the Mir Space Station from Endeavour

◀ Skylab was the final mission of Saturn V, the rocket that carried the famous Moon-landing missions

▶ Astronauts floating in zero gravity inside the ISS

Living in Space

As you can imagine, living in outer space is vastly different from living on Earth. The atmosphere, gravity, warmth, water, regular day-and-night cycles and even the freedom to move about are simply not possible in space. Large teams of people have been working to recreate the well-being of life on Earth for astronauts in space vehicles and stations.

◀ *Astronauts on the ISS rise from their sleeping quarters on Christmas morning in 2010*

🔍 Mental Fitness

Cosmonauts on the early space stations like Salyut and Mir were the first to show signs of mental stress from extended stays in outer space. Their experience led the Russians to set up studies in aerospace psychology. In the mid-1990s, Russian space psychologists shared their insights with NASA. Today's aerospace psychologists ensure that the people going up to space possess strong, sturdy minds. They also support the astronauts throughout training, the mission and in adjusting to life after the mission.

👤 In Real Life

On the ISS, astronauts can watch DVDs and talk to their families once a week.

▲ *Mealtime aboard the ISS*

🔍 Zero Gravity

In space, a body has no weight. Astronauts simply float from one place to another. Without any work to do, their back and legs quickly lose muscle density. Even the heart, which is a muscle, shrinks in size. Without the need for a strong skeleton, bones lose calcium, which forms stones in the kidneys. Blood and body fluids settle in the upper body (instead of flowing downwards). This makes astronauts puffy and congested, as if they have a bad cold. Since the absence of gravity means that there is no 'up' or 'down' in space, most astronauts get space-sick. They suffer from nausea, headaches and even find it hard to locate their own limbs! To minimise these issues, astronauts exercise regularly while in space.

▶ *Astronaut Marsha Ivins in zero-gravity outer space*

◀ *ESA astronaut Frank De Winne exercising on a special treadmill in the ISS*

From Food to Waste

Early astronauts took their food in the form of food cubes, dehydrated meals or mush in aluminium tubes. Nowadays, they have a choice of 150 different types of food. Brushing teeth is very similar to what you do on Earth. Except, there are no sinks that let out water, so astronauts spit into a washcloth. They also use washcloths with special soaps and shampoos to clean their bodies without water. It is impossible to do laundry in space, so they take along several sets of underwear! On the Space Shuttle, there are four trash bins with trash liners that are sealed as soon as they are full.

▲ Food for astronauts comes in various forms

▲ The toilet on board the Zvezda space module

▶ Astronaut Cady Coleman washing her hair with special shampoo on the space station

Incredible Individuals

Cosmonaut Anatoly Solovyev holds the record for the most spacewalks. He undertook 16 of them.

▲ Astronaut Anatoly Solovyev suiting up for a space walk

Spacesuits

When astronauts leave a spacecraft, they do so wearing a protective spacesuit. It is made of interchangeable parts that can be adjusted to fit various sizes. The suit is made of modern materials like Ortho-Fabric and aluminised Mylar, to which metal parts are attached. It is puncture-proof and equipped with cameras, drinking-water and even a diaper-like pouch to contain urine. Inventors began building full-pressure suits for extreme altitudes in the 1930s. The first one to be worn in outer space was the Soviet SK-1 suit, worn by Yuri Gagarin.

The Future of Space Exploration

With so many agencies focused on space exploration, the frontiers of human existence are being steadily pushed outwards. Private enterprises like SpaceX and Mars One are even concentrating on colonising Mars. With space probes discovering water, atmosphere and other conditions conducive to life out there, human presence on alien planets may soon be a reality.

Star Wars

Spy satellites and anti-satellite weapons are already a modern-day reality. In the 1950s, the US even considered bombing the Moon to display their technological might. Since then, many countries have developed their own nuclear weapons and missile capabilities. In the late 60s, the US, UK and Soviet Union entered into an Outer Space Treaty. This laid out principles for exploration and use of outer space and celestial bodies. For instance, it specifies that no weapons testing, or military actions can be carried out on the Moon or on any celestial body. As of February 2019, over 100 countries have signed this treaty, which forms the basis for international space law. While the treaty bans weapons of mass destruction, it sadly does not prevent the use of conventional weapons in space.

Space Tourism

As reusable rockets and cheaper rocket technology come into existence, large-scale space tourism could really take off in the near future. The Russian space agency has already taken tourists to Earth's orbit. In 2001, American multimillionaire Dennis Tito paid to visit outer space and became the first space tourist. He spent close to eight days in orbit. In 1985, Christa McAuliffe, a school teacher, was chosen to fly to space; tragically, she was put on board the disastrous Challenger mission. In 2006, the Iranian-American engineer Anousheh Ansari became the first female space tourist.

▶ In the 1990s, eight people were asked to live in the isolated Biosphere-2 habitat for two long years, so scientists could understand the needs of human beings who might colonise a new world

▶ Ever since Chandrayaan-1 discovered lunar water, there is renewed interest in establishing a colony on the Moon

🔍 Colonising Space

Many people believe that it is necessary to colonise other planets, in case Earth is destroyed by natural disasters—or through human greed and recklessness! Many enterprises have been set up with this goal in mind. No human beings have landed on another planet yet. So, we are still a long way from creating the controlled living environment needed for colonisation and survival. As interplanetary robotic probes send back more information from the solar system, our scientists are steadily developing the large-scale technologies that will be needed to power human life in an alien world.

▲ *Anousheh Ansari with a grass plant on board the ISS*

⊙ Incredible Individuals

The billionaire and founder of Cirque du Soleil, Guy Laliberte is also an accordion player, a fire-eater and a stilt-walker. In 2009, he became Canada's first space tourist on a mission to raise awareness about water issues on our planet. This was the first social mission to space.

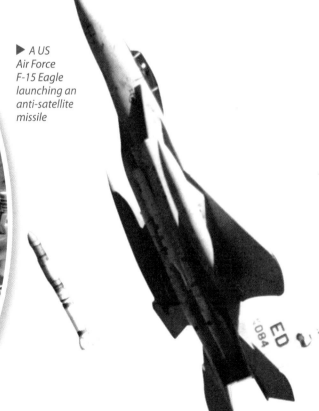

▲ *Guy Laliberte (centre) along with American and Russian astronauts waving farewell before taking off on their flight to the ISS*

▶ *A US Air Force F-15 Eagle launching an anti-satellite missile*

Word Check

Aperture: In telescopes and cameras, aperture refers to the hole through which light travels to reach the instrument and our eyes (or camera film).

Astronomers: They are people who make systematic observations and records of celestial objects.

Astrophysics: It is the study of the stars and all other celestial bodies. It also combines theories and laws with observations of the universe.

Cosmology: It is the study of the universe, its formation, evolution and future.

Escape velocity: It is the minimum speed needed to break free from the gravitational pull of a massive body. For instance, a rocket needs to travel at an escape velocity of about 11.186 kmps to get away from Earth.

Exoplanet: Also known as extrasolar planets, they are planets that orbit a star other than the Sun.

Gamma rays, X-rays and infrared rays: They are different types of electromagnetic rays; they are like light rays, but are invisible to our eyes.

Geostationary: It refers to the orbit of a satellite that keeps up with the spin of Earth; thus, it remains above the same spot in comparison to our planet.

Heliocentrism: It is the model of the universe where the Sun is at the centre of the solar system and the other planets revolve around it.

Heliosphere: It is a massive bubble-like region around the Sun formed by solar wind.

Impactor: It is a craft that is sent out specifically to collide with a celestial object.

Interstellar space: It is the space within a galaxy that is beyond the influence of its individual stars.

Ions: They are atoms with extra electrons or missing electrons.

Lander: It is a space module that lands on celestial bodies such as asteroids, comets, planets and natural satellites.

Plasma: It is the fourth state of matter (after solid, liquid and gas); it is an ionized gas.

Precession: It describes the motion of a body spinning in such a way that it wobbles, so that the axis of rotation sweeps out a cone.